Snapchat Marketing Table of Contents

Introduction: Why Snapchat Marketing? 4
    Snapchat Is All about the Next Generation 5
    Snapchat Creates Excitement.. 5
    Snapchat Can Increase Your Online Presence and Gain You New Followers 6
Chapter One: What exactly is Snapchat?.. 7
    How Snapchat Works... 8
    What's the Point of Snapchat?... 9
Chapter Two: Getting Your Brand on Snapchat 10
    Signing up... 11
    Email Address 11
    Password and Date of Birth... 11
    Your Phone Number 12
    Verification Code 12
    Your Profile and Logo 12
Chapter Three: Using Snapchat – The Basics 13
    Navigation 14
Chapter Four: Using Snapchat – Features Businesses Use the Most 16
    Your Logo and QR Code 17
Chapter Five: Using Snapchat – Advanced Features 19
    Using Zoom in Your Videos 20
    Using Your Own Photos 20
    Improving Your Snaps and Videos 20
Chapter Six: Introduction to Marketing on Snapchat... 23
    Setting Your Account so Everyone Can View Your Stories 24
Chapter Seven: Getting Your Initial Following.. 26
    Let Your Creativity Free 27
    Use Your Other Social Networks.. 27
    Put Your Snapcode Everywhere... 27
    Use Social Media Influencers.. 28
    Things Not to Do to Get Followers on Snapchat 28

Chapter Eight: Building Fans through Stories 29
  Creating Amazing Stories 30
Chapter Nine: Discover – Snapchat's Partner Program 32
Chapter Ten: Viewing Statistics 34
Chapter Eleven: Using Snapchat at Live Events to get Followers 38
Chapter Twelve: Using Snapchat to Deliver Personal Content 40
Chapter Thirteen: Give Followers an Inside Look 43
Chapter Fourteen: Running Contests & Promotions on Snapchat 46
  Designing Your Promotion 47
  Promoting Your Promotion 47
  Checking Your Contest Entries 47
Chapter Fifteen: Aligning Yourself with Niche Influencers on Snapchat 49
  What are Niche Influencers? 50
  Benefits of Using Niche Influencers 50
  How to Use Niche Influencers 51
  How to Find Niche Influencers 51
Chapter Sixteen: Measuring Your Success with Snapchat 52
  First, Let's Talk about the Numbers 53
  Now, Let's Talk about the Demographics 53
  Now, Let's Talk about User Response 54
Chapter Seventeen: Learning From Other Brands on Snapchat 55
  News Articles 56
  Ask Other People in the Industry 56
  Follow Marketing Blogs That Are All about the Trends 57
Chapter Eighteen: Integrating Snapchat with Your Site & Social Media 58
Conclusion: 61

Introduction:

THE INTRODUCTION GIVES YOU DETAILS ON WHY YOU SHOULD CHOOSE SNAPCHAT MARKETING FOR YOUR BUSINESS.

Introduction: Why Snapchat Marketing?

If you want to be in business for the long run and stay relevant, you are going to need to keep tabs on the social media landscape and join social networks that are going to take you into the future. That's exactly what Snapchat does. This platform is one of the social media outlets that have come from a constantly evolving world of social media and it uses a novel and never-before-seen method of communicating – a way of communicating that shows where the future of social media is headed.

Snapchat Is All about the Next Generation

Do you want one really great reason to join Snapchat? There are way more than one but if you need just one, think about the fact that Snapchat has become one of the most popular social media applications for people aged 12 to 24 years old. As you can see, that means that the next generation of buyers and the generation after that are all going to be potential Snapchat veterans and if your brand is on Snapchat and has been from the beginning, there is a good chance that you're reaching a lot of these young people.

Snapchat Creates Excitement

Another great reason to join is that the way that Snapchat works is extremely fun and promotes serious interactivity between users. Snapchat is an exciting way to use social media and brands are capitalizing on these young people's desire for exciting content by providing them with things like behind-the-scenes information about an event or brand, special promotions, discounts or giveaways that they couldn't find out about from any other source. Because of the way that information is communicated and how quickly it disappears, Snapchat promotes excitement with every single post.

Snapchat Can Increase Your Online Presence and Gain You New Followers

Snapchat is also a great way to increase your online presence. You may already have profiles on websites like Twitter and Facebook, and you probably have a Pinterest account and other social media as well. But whenever you join a major social media network you're going to be expanding your online presence and you will gain followers all around as a result, as well as retain followers better on your other social media networks. In fact, you will have a significant number of people coming to follow you on Snapchat from your other social media profiles as well as having people find that your Twitter and Facebook because they followed you on Snapchat.

No matter how you slice it, Snapchat is one very possible future of social media. Making sure that you are prepared for the next generation of buyers is something that every business should be doing and when you see a social media platform like Snapchat that is gaining popularity so fast – to the tune of 200 million active users per month – you need to get involved as quickly as possible and start using it to build your business even bigger.

Chapter 1:

WHAT EXACTLY IS SNAPCHAT?

Chapter One: What exactly is Snapchat?

Snapchat is a very powerful social media platform that has become very popular as of late. Major brands are not only starting to get their presence onto Snapchat but also advertise on the platform through Snapchat's discovery system. Snapchat is similar to other social media applications in that you create a profile and then have followers or fans that you communicate with. However, that is pretty much the extent of the similarities. Snapchat is remarkably different in the way that users communicate with each other and in the ways that information is shared.

How Snapchat Works

Snapchat is a program that works with a very specific media for communicating with other users. There are a couple of differences that make this program unique and one of the most interesting social media platforms in use today like using photos and videos to communicate with other people. While Twitter, Facebook and most social media platforms mainly communicate with text, the only text that you will find here is the captions on pictures and videos. Another difference was Snapchat is that when you post your pictures and videos they will only last from 1 to 10 seconds with just a single exception, which we'll get into later.

It might be difficult to understand how this works if you've never used the application. Just imagine that someone you are following on social media posts something and you get an alert. You go to their feed and check what they have posted and it is either a picture with a caption or a short video, or if you didn't get there fast enough, you missed out. That's basically how Snapchat works and you have followers and friends on the platform just like you do with other social media websites.

What's the Point of Snapchat?

Snapchat is leading the way into the future of social media. This platform is going to be one of the big ones that will serve the next generation of consumers. The app is already being used by most teenagers and even Facebook has seen the value of Snapchat and offered $3 billion for the company. However, the creators of Snapchat believed in their company enough that they refused Facebook's offer. Facebook has people who analyze a great deal of data in order to predict future trends and if they think Snapchat is valuable then brands should be jumping on as quickly as they can.

So, what's the point of Snapchat? To socialize. To build a following. To communicate with other people who share interests with you or have an emotional investment in what you are posting. On one hand, Snapchat is just a social media platform but on the other hand it may be the application which leads the charge into the future where social media posts will be less text and more pictures and video. Brands like Mashable, National Geographic and Comedy Central as well as several dozen others see enough value in Snapchat to advertise with the application as part of the discovery feature and thousands of others have joined the platform as well. If you have a brand – it should be on Snapchat.

Chapter 2:

GETTING YOUR BRAND ON SNAPCHAT

Chapter Two: Getting Your Brand on Snapchat

The first thing that you're going to need to do if you want to reap the benefits of the Snapchat application is get your brand onto the platform. This chapter will explain exactly what you need to do to create your Snapchat account and how to fill out your profile information correctly so that your Snapchat is ready to use and you can start getting followers and marketing your brand in new and interesting ways.

Signing up

Obviously, the first thing that you're going to want to do is download the Snapchat application. You can add this app to either your Android or your iOS device. There is no support for Windows operating systems as of yet or any of the lesser-known ones. Once you have Snapchat downloaded on your phone or mobile device, launch it and you'll be taken to a screen where it will ask you to either sign in or sign up. You are going to sign up with the following information:

Email Address

You want to use an email address that you actually check. In fact, this may be a good time to use your main email address – or the one for your business. Whatever you do, don't just make one up because you will have to verify your account.

Password and Date of Birth

The next thing that you'll enter is your password and your date of birth. There aren't many restrictions with your password and you should have no problem entering one. Your date of birth is also easy, using the date tool that comes with most mobile devices.

Your Phone Number

The last thing that you'll enter is your phone number. You want to enter your valid mobile number because they are going to send you a verification code that you'll have to enter into the app to use it fully.

Verification Code

They're going to send you the verification code but you may not be able to enter it into the app without some help navigating to the right place. Since we are going to get into navigation in a later chapter, and explain where everything is, for now just know that the place you enter your verification code is under the gear icon that opens the settings menu.

Your Profile and Logo

Snapchat doesn't have a place for you to fill out your profile like Twitter and Facebook and other social media platforms do. In fact, you can't even upload your logo from the app. The only thing that you can do if you want to customize your profile picture from the app is take a picture of either your face or a picture of your logo and customize it that way. The problem with this method is that it doesn't look professional and sense Snapchat takes a series of five pictures, quickly in a row to make an animated GIF, it is impossible to hold your hand steady enough to get a decent picture, even if you have a high quality camera.

For brands, this is just unacceptable. However, there is a way to get your profile photo to be your logo and to insert it digitally, so that it is as high-quality as possible. We will get into that in Chapter Four.

Chapter 3:

USING SNAPCHAT – THE BASICS

Chapter Three: Using Snapchat – The Basics

Now that you've signed up for a Snapchat and your brand is on the app, you are going to need to know how to use the application. In this chapter, we're only going to go over the basics – the things you need to know to get around and check out the some of the buttons and knobs. In subsequent chapters, we will cover more advanced features and some things in further detail, including some of the features the businesses are going to be using the most.

Navigation

The first thing that you need to know is how to navigate Snapchat successfully. So go to your app and open it and follow along as we discuss how you navigate through the Snapchat interface. When you enter the application, the first thing you'll see is your camera, either facing you are facing away from you, depending on what you've set it at. It is very easy to change the camera view. If you wanted to take a selfie instead a picture of what is in front of you, all you do is touch the little smiley face surrounded by arrows in the top right of your camera screen. Is very easy to hit this accidentally, which is why you may see your camera facing front are facing you when you login.

Navigating is done with swipes. If you swipe right you will see your contacts list, which is probably just team Snapchat right now. You can tap on the little speech bubble at the top right corner of the screen to chat with your contacts and you can search them by touching the magnifying glass. This is particularly useful if you have lots and lots of people in your contact list and you need to find a specific person.

If you swipe left you will see the stories that have been posted. The major brands – or the ones that have become a Snapchat partner on the top row while the other stories are from live events under the word 'live.'

If you swipe down from your home screen you will see your Snapchat QR code which is the yellow icon with the ghost in the middle. Those dots that you see there send a message to mobile devices of users that want to follow you and make it very easy to follow someone. This is one of the revolutionary new methods of adding followers the Snapchat is come up with. As you can see there are several features on here. You see your trophies for example, see who added you and add other people and then get a list of your friends.

You also notice that there is a gear icon in the top right corner. Tapping this will allow you to view your personal information and if you scroll down you'll see the login verification setting. This is where you will enter the code that they sent you via your mobile device. If you chose not to add a phone number they have you solve a puzzle instead to prove that you're human being.

That is all are going to cover for now. We will get into the more advanced features in the next couple chapters. If you are a brand and you want a quick start help guide to get you on Snapchat as quickly as possible, the next chapter covers the features that businesses need to know.

Chapter 4:

USING SNAPCHAT – FEATURES BUSINESSES USE THE MOST

Chapter Four: Using Snapchat – Features Businesses Use the Most

As mentioned in the last chapter, we are now going to go over a couple of the features that businesses use the most, namely the logo and QR code. This is intended as sort of a quick start process. The basics in the last chapter were intended to get you navigating around the application successfully and this chapter will demonstrate how to use your QR code and a workaround for the lack of ability to upload your brand's logo to your profile directly.

Your Logo and QR Code

Adding your logo to your Snapchat is going to take some creativity. That's because Snapchat doesn't allow you to upload a logo. What it does allow you to do is take up picture – which is actually a series of five pictures taken one right after the other – of your face or whatever you want. So, you can take a picture of your logo and it will be on your Snapchat profile and QR code. You should either find a way to take a picture with the camera that is perfectly still – and very high quality – or come up with some creative way to take a picture of your logo with the five snapshots which will be strung together to make a short GIF.

As for your QR code, it is intended to be something that you share in the real world and allow people to take pictures of to add you on Snapchat. You can add your logo to your QR code image that you have to be careful doing it so that you don't mess up the code embedded within the dots that allows Snapchat to recognize your brand from that QR code.

The first thing that you're going to do is [download your QR code](#), which requires you to go to that link (which is the Snapchat website), login to your Snapchat account and then download your QR code. Then, you can either take it into Photoshop yourself (and Photoshop is recommended for this particular project because of the layers function) and magically erase the white ghost and then put your logo on the layer below it so that it can be seen through the transparency of the ghost. You could also find someone on Fiverr to do it for you if you don't have Photoshop or don't want to use it. There are some pretty specific guidelines that you need to follow however, and if you're outsourcing this project, make sure that you share these with the person.

- Do not alter the shape of the ghost and do not break the black border. (Or remove it) around the ghost. This will cause your QR code to fail and people will not be able to use it to follow you on Snapchat.
- Don't stretch the box and anyway for change the shape of it.
- Don't invert the colors to try to be different.
- Do not print on glossy paper or cardstock because the shine may prevent people from those days, scanning your code.

Then, you just put up the QR code anywhere you want – your website, social media platforms and everywhere online, but also in the real world. You can have the QR code blown up and posted on the wall at your brick-and-mortar store(s), you can even put it on your business cards. You might even be able to put it on a billboard or on the side of company vehicles, but you should test that thoroughly before spending any significant amount of money on it.

There are other features that businesses use, such as the story feature, but we're going to get into that subject in Chapters Six and Eight.

Chapter 5:

USING SNAPCHAT – ADVANCED FEATURES

Chapter Five: Using Snapchat – Advanced Features

In this chapter, we're going to go over some of the more advanced features of Snapchat. We're going to skip things that will be covered in later chapters like stories but this chapter will allow you to use the basic functions of Snapchat like the videos and pictures to get you started in the platform's world.

Using Zoom in Your Videos

You don't have to take a standard picture or video with Snapchat. By default, the videos is zoomed all the way out but all you have to do to zoom in is use two fingers and pull them apart just like if you are zooming in on a webpage on your phone. Zooming out is the opposite; bring your fingers together. One other small side note: if you haven't found it yet, the control to flip your camera from front-facing to rear-facing is on the top right of your video screen.

Using Your Own Photos

In case you didn't know, you can use the photos that are in your phone's library to use in one-to-one communication in a direct message. All you do is swipe right on any friend that you want to send a picture to and tap on the blue bubble at the left side of the screen when it comes in the frame. Your private chat will open with them and you can tap on the yellow circle like you're getting ready to take a picture, and when your camera comes up, look at the bottom right where you will see the last photo that you took and you can tap on it and open your library. Then insert whatever photo from your library you want and share it as a snap.

Improving Your Snaps and Videos

You probably already know that you can add a caption to your picture video. After all, the app sometimes asks you if you want to leave a caption when you click the shutter button; (if it doesn't, you can click the 'T' at the top). But did you know there are actually ways that you can improve your caption? Here are the ways that you can make your snaps and videos look amazing.

You can change the size of your caption text as well as the placement. All you have to do is after you type your caption, type the 'T' a second time and it will make your text much larger and thicker. If you tap it again, it will center your text. If you want to make your text even bigger then use the same spreading your fingers motion that you used to zoom and make it as big as you like. Make sure that you put each finger on the end of the text; it may take a few practice tries. You can then experiment with moving the text around and resizing it to create anything you want.

You probably saw the icon that looks like a piece of paper to the left of the text icon, and the one on the right that looks like a pencil or pen. The one on the left is the comprehensive list of emojis that Snapchat has to offer. You can choose an emoji, and then resize it just like you did with the text as well as move it around, rotate it or anything you like. If you tap on the pencil icon at allows you to choose a color and then write with your finger (or a stylus if you have one) on your snap. You can find a list of the emojis and what they mean online.

Another thing that you can do is go to your settings menu and turn on geofilters. All you do is go down to additional services and tap manage and it will allow you to enable filters. Once you have done this you can go back to your picture and it will ask you – or rather tell you – that you can swipe right for filters. Filters differ with each geographical zone which is why Snapchat asked for your ZIP Code when you enable them. Go through the filters that are available and see if there any you like.

There are a couple of neat things that you can do that we will end the chapter with. First, if you tap on the words in your caption you will notice that tapping on one word will underline it then you can tap the word and hold and it will highlight it. Then you can change the color of that individual word to whatever you want. This is particularly useful if you want to use letters as frames. You can play with this and find what works best for you but an example is making the 'O' large enough to where most of it is out of frame and the part that is left frames your picture in an oval. Finally, another advanced feature that you should know about is that once per day you can replay someone's snap. However, it has to be the last snap that you viewed. You will see the option to replay on your screen after the snap expires.

Chapter 6:

INTRODUCTION TO MARKETING ON SNAPCHAT

Chapter Six: Introduction to Marketing on Snapchat

Marketing on Snapchat is a little unusual and it is centered around the story feature. We will get into the actual construction of stories in Chapter 8; the purpose of this chapter is to show you how you market with stories.

The first thing you should know is what a story actually is. That requires understanding a little bit of Snapchat terminology if you haven't already learned it. A snap is a video or picture that you send a specific person. Although you certainly can advertise with snaps, they are only going to one person at a time and they disappear in no more than 10 seconds. This makes it an almost unusable marketing tool – even if it were lucrative to send snaps to your existing friends list. Of course, it's not lucrative and that's the point. So, we won't worry about snaps in this chapter.

However, we *are* going to discuss stories. The difference between a story and a snap is that stories contain multiple images and video and stay available for viewing for 24 hours. The other difference is that while you can send snaps to just people on your friends list (or the rare person that is enabled everyone to send them snaps) you stories can be viewed by anyone you choose. You can set your account to allow anyone to view your stories. Since stories can be shared, they are a great marketing strategy.

Setting Your Account so Everyone Can View Your Stories

This is something, as you may have guessed, that can be done in your settings menu. So swipe down and when you get to the page where it allows you to see who has added you, click on the settings gear at the top right. Then go down to where you can change both who can send you snaps and who can view your stories.

So now you are ready to start sharing stories on Snapchat. You may not know how to build a story yet, but that's okay because are going to cover that in Chapter 8. Make sure that you let other social media networks know when you post a story because you will have Snapchat users on those networks and they will log in and check out your story. If your story is geared towards some sort of product or service you definitely want as many people viewing it as possible, so don't rely on just Snapchat to get views. However, keep in mind to always be entertaining so that users will want to share your story with others, and will come back for the next one.

Chapter 7:

GETTING YOUR INITIAL FOLLOWING

Chapter Seven: Getting Your Initial Following

If you want to be successful in marketing on Snapchat then you're going to need to get a following. Just like with your Twitter and Facebook followers, the more people that you have following you, the higher the chances that other people will follow you. This chapter will give you some tips on getting your first followers on Snapchat as well as some things not to do to get followers.

Let Your Creativity Free

The first thing that you want to do is make sure that anything that you're posting is creative and fun and shows off your artistic expressions. Posting boring content with text that is always the same never changes, over the same boring videos of products are going to get exactly nowhere with Snapchat. But pictures of people using your product in unconventional ways, with your caption and emojis, is going to get people's interest and make them want to share your content.

Use Your Other Social Networks

We discussed this a little bit in the last chapter but it might be useful to understand exactly how you should use your social networks to get Snapchat followers. The best way to do it is to come up with compelling things to post on your Twitter, Facebook, Instagram or whatever social network you're using. These are teaser items such as a promo code within the story that you can only get if you go to Snapchat.

Put Your Snapcode Everywhere

Place your snapcode or Snapchat information anywhere that you can. Post it on your website, around your store if you have one and anywhere else that you can think of where people that you want to influence would be willing to join Snapchat or are already using it. You also put it on your business cards, put a link to it in your email or even advertise on forums that are in your industry.

Use Social Media Influencers

Do you know a YouTuber or someone who has a large following online but isn't necessarily Hollywood celebrity? Do you think they are someone that would be interested in your product or service? You might be able to leverage influencers by offering them something special which they will almost always talk about afterward and you can get followers from that.

Things Not to Do to Get Followers on Snapchat

There are a few things that you shouldn't do to get followers on Snapchat. One of them is to use one of the services offered on websites like Fiverr that promise to get you thousands of followers. For one thing, they are not going to buy anything from you and may not even have real people behind them. Also, you might get your Snapchat account banned by doing so at some point in the future. You also should try not to be boring and make sure that you're accessible in some way because users don't want a shadowy face in the background, they want a real live human being behind your company that they can interact with.

Chapter 8:

BUILDING FANS THROUGH STORIES

Chapter Eight: Building Fans through Stories

You're going to use stories to do more than advertise your products or services. Think of a story like a viral video. You know if you make it overly promotional it's not going to work. You want something clever, something that no one has ever seen and something that evokes emotion in a human being. This will make them want to share with their friends and it will give you the exposure that you're looking for. But creating good stories will also make people want to follow you so every time you create a story keep in mind that you are both trying to get people to follow you and you're trying to get your product or service out there.

Creating Amazing Stories

If you want to know how to create a great Snapchat story then go online and look at some of the best ones that have ever been made. There are lots of Snapchat stories that have been featured on websites like Buzzfeed, Mashable or even some of the more conventional media out there. As you look through those Snapchat stories and laugh, try to think of ways in which you can incorporate a similar campaign on your own Snapchat account that would both be entertaining and promote your product or service a little.

Stories can not only be told in photos, they can also include video. You can come up with a clever idea to pair the video with the snapshots if you like. There are lots of ways to create a good story but it starts with a good idea. Sit down with employees or even your friends and try to come up with a Snapchat story that would be funny. Use anything for inspiration; go to Google search and type in a random word and look at the images that come up with that word. Look around your environment and see if there's anything there that amuses you. Think about the last thing that you found funny and why you liked it. There are lots of ways to come up with great ideas for stories.

Sit down and storyboard out your story, which means that you decide which order your snaps and videos are going to go in, before you even take them in some cases, and then make sure that you have the right order and a compelling story that is going to keep people clicking the next button. Remember, just like with YouTube videos, you shouldn't go over a few minutes in length. Otherwise, people are going to get bored. Now, you can get to work making great stories on Snapchat!

Chapter 9:

SNAPCHAT'S PARTNER PROGRAM

Chapter Nine: Discover – Snapchat's Partner Program

One thing you may be interested in knowing about is Snapchat's partner program called Discover. This program is pretty much out of reach for anyone who isn't a major brand because of the $750,000 (per day) price tag, but there are actually other ways to get on Discover then by being a partner with Snapchat.

Some of the major brands are letting other brands advertise on their Discover space for a lot less than they are paying for their Discover spot. This is a way for the brands that are advertising on Discover to get some of the money back that they are spending and it is a great way for anyone with about $50,000 to spend to get a huge amount of exposure.

For smaller brands, unfortunately there is nothing yet that they can do to start advertising with Snapchat. There would have to be some sort of major overhaul to the application if they were going to start allowing people to advertise on snaps and videos and other places around the site. Right now, there is nothing that is the equivalent of Facebook advertising for small businesses and people with products or services to promote but that may be coming in the future. Snapchat has only recently been able to get enough followers to command the kind of rates that they are getting from their Discover program.

So the bottom line here is, if you have a great deal of money to spend on advertising then Snapchat may be exactly what you need – or at least advertising on one of the brands that are currently on or will be on Snapchat's Discover program in the near future. If you have a small business or you just want to advertise products and services, then you should use Snapchat for marketing purposes in the ways that we discussed in this book rather than advertising on the platform.

Chapter 10:

VIEWING STATISTICS

Chapter Ten: Viewing Statistics

Another thing that you're going to want to do what it comes to Snapchat is find out what kind of statistics you can get and how you can use them to make your brand better. Unfortunately Snapchat doesn't really offer any sort of detailed analytics or anything to tell you who is visiting your story page, but it does have some statistics that you might find useful. In this article were going to go over those as well as tell you about the alternatives that are cropping up that may give you the analytics information that you need.

There are several metrics that Snapchat offers you. The first one that we're going to discuss here is the total unique views that a story has gotten – and stories are the only analytics that we will discuss here because that's what you will be using as a marketer and also it is the only feature on the site that Snapchat offers analytics on.

Total unique views tell you how many people opened up your story and saw at least the first frame. They may not of gone on to finish the story and in fact may not have even when past that first frame but it tells you how many people opened up your story and it is very accurate. The thing about stories is that you can see how many views are on every single frame of the story – or on the video if you created a video – and that's how you get these total unique views – you go to the first frame and look.

The second analytic that were going to discuss is total story completions. You get your total story completions by going to the very last frame of your story and taking a look how many people finished your story. Make sure that you're keeping track of these metrics as you see them and also keep in mind is this will be after the 24 hours that your story has been live.

The third analytic is probably the most important of all of these and it's the completion rate which you'll figure out yourself by looking at your total unique views compared to your total story completions. So for example, if you had 1000 people start your story but only 450 completed it you would have a 45% completion rate; the higher that your rate is, the better your story.

Finally, the fourth analytic that were going to discuss is the stopping point. You want to look at your snaps and try to figure out if there is a trend as to when they stopped watching or viewing your story. If you can detect a trend at a certain frame then you will have discovered where the problem was – which means the problem was somewhere up to that point not necessarily the frame that they stopped on.

Companies That Are Providing Analytics Information

There are a few companies out there that are providing analytics information for Snapchat. They have only popped up recently, but they have some innovative programs and several have very good reputations with businesses that are looking to market on Snapchat. If you want to find out what is going on with your Snapchat account and have detailed analytics so that you can make the best decisions possible on what to post and when as well as what's working and what isn't, then you might want to look into using one of these companies. Just do your research and make sure that other people are recommending the service and that the price isn't outrageous compared to the going rate.

Chapter 11:

USING SNAPCHAT AT LIVE EVENTS TO GET FOLLOWERS

Chapter Eleven: Using Snapchat at Live Events to get Followers

In this chapter, were going to discuss a couple of ways that you can use live events to get followers to your Snapchat account. The first thing that you should do is open up your Snapchat app and look where the Discover page is. You will see a place where it says live and then you will find stories below that. Don't get confused by this live event feature that Snapchat has.

They do a thing called Our Story where they pick a live event that's going on and then take people's snaps and video from that event and build a curated story that everyone can see regardless of who they are following. That is not the type of live event that will be discussing in this chapter. The type of live event that you want to use Snapchat for is the kind of live event where your company is doing something exciting that customers can attend. You can hold these events whenever you like, and you can use Snapchat to both bring people to your live event and convince people that are already at your live event to sign up and follow you on Snapchat.

The way that you get people from your Snapchat to your live event is fairly straightforward. Just build a story using snaps in that event and invite people out. Just remember, stories last for 24 hours so the best way for you to do a live event with Snapchat stories is have the story begin before the live event starts – 24 hours before the start of your event. Then you can start a brand-new story when the event starts and people will be able to check out live images and video from the event.

Obviously, this is a great way to get people to your event because you not only get people that have to prepare for the event and are willing to come 24 hours after hearing about it, but you also get people who are more of right-here-right-now, fly by the seat of your pants people. In other words, people who will come to your live event on very short notice.

It is worth noting that this will only work if you have followers in the same city that you are doing the event in and if you are a large brand and you are in a large city this is usually not a problem. For small businesses, many of their followers will have followed them by coming into their brick-and-mortar store and so they will not have a problem either. In fact, the only people who are going to have a problem are the people who do not have a brick-and-mortar store and only work online but have a very small business and not a huge Snapchat following. Holding a live event will be very poorly attended because very few of your Snapchat followers are likely to be in that particular area.

In either case, whether you are convincing people to sign up and follow you on Snapchat from your live event, or you are trying to convince followers in that area to come to your live event, you should definitely use some sort of promotion, coupon or giveaway to entice them.

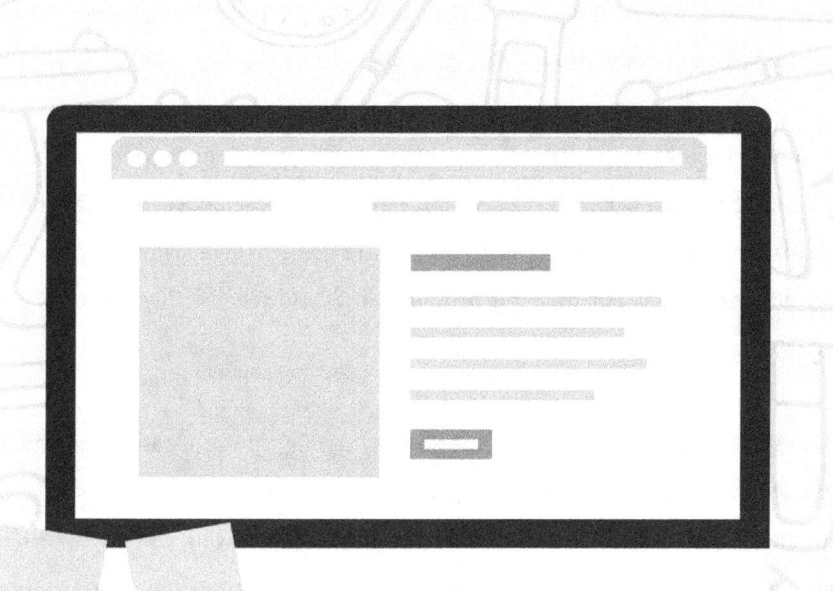

Chapter 12:

USING SNAPCHAT TO DELIVER PERSONAL CONTENT

Chapter Twelve: Using Snapchat to Deliver Personal Content

This chapter is designed to give you some ideas on how you can deliver personal content to the people who follow you on Snapchat, including what kind of content you can deliver and some ideas for some great personal deliveries, as well as tips on how you should deliver them.

This is something that you would do individually with your followers and is designed to work with a promotion that you have going on. For example, suppose that you posted on your website that sometime in the next few days you are going to give away a certain number of free items or gift certificates but that the people who would receive them would be followers on Snapchat whom you sent a personal snap to.

What you should do next, is choose a specific day during that week and even choose the hours that you will be doing it between. Then you can ramp up your advertising efforts a little during that period because you know that the people that are following you on Snapchat are paying attention because they want to get a free item and they will read your stories more frequently. This is just one way that delivering personal content can help your business.

Another way that you can use personal contact to grow your business is by thanking customers when they purchase something from your website by sending them a snap and then create a story with those snaps. This is a great method because all it requires is that you asked people on your order form to put in their Snapchat ID.

There are many different ways out there of using personal communication to grow your business. You can try to get referrals from the people who are currently following you by creating a story that tells them that they will get something at a huge discount or for free if they can get a certain number of people to follow you on Snapchat. You may have to have them post on another social media network – Twitter is the best option – because you may not see it on

Snapchat if they snap and send you the name of a user that followed you based on their recommendation. You can ask them to post the person's Snapchat ID on Twitter with a specific hashtag and then you can check your Snapchat followers to find out if that person has joined that day and then you can then give them credit for the follow.

Chapter 13:

GIVE FOLLOWERS AN INSIDE LOOK

Chapter Thirteen: Give Followers an Inside Look

Another great way that you can use Snapchat is to provide your followers with some behind-the-scenes information or an inside look at something that you're doing. This has a number of benefits, first and foremost being that the people who follow you on Snapchat will pay closer attention to your snaps and stories and will keep your business in mind if they need your product or service because you are already in their mind. But another benefit is that if you're behind the scenes information is exciting, and whatever you're building or doing is compelling, people are going to want to share it.

There are lots of ways that you can use this. First of all, make sure that all of the other social media you use knows that you're posting exclusive scenes information on Snapchat. That means that if the followers from your other social media platforms want to see the behind-the-scenes information, they are going to become followers on Snapchat as well, which gives you more followers. You can use this several ways to get followers every time you have something that you can show behind the scenes information of.

You can even drive traffic to your own website using Snapchat. If you snap and build stories you can place a method for getting to your website within the story as well as a reason for them to go there – a call to action that is going to give them some sort of benefit. You always want to make sure that you have some sort of benefit to offer them. One great way to use Snapchat to get some long-term results is to direct them to your website and have them sign up for your mailing list. That means that you can now send emails and people will look at an email much longer than they will a tweet or a snap story most of the time.

The main thing here is that you just make sure that you are always interacting with your audience. If you have something that you think that would be great on Snapchat, make sure you put it on there. Make sure that you take every opportunity that you have to give people that follow you on social media some sort of inside information about your company or something that they didn't have before. If you want them to do something and follow a call to action, then make sure that you are offering some sort of benefit to do so as well.

Chapter 14:

RUNNING CONTESTS & PROMOTIONS ON SNAPCHAT

Chapter Fourteen: Running Contests & Promotions on Snapchat

Snapchat is a great place to run contests and promotions. Many of the other businesses that are on Snapchat use this method to both say thanks – usually with discounts – and to get more followers by stirring up some excitement. So, how do you run a contest or promotion that will do well on Snapchat? In this chapter, we'll explore some of the ways that you can use this type of marketing on Snapchat and some of the benefits that you can get from it.

Designing Your Promotion

The first thing you're going to have to do is design your promotion. You need to figure out what kind of things are going to require from the customers or followers and how you are going to set it up logistically. For example, they could add you as a friend on Snapchat and then you could request them to create a video or take a snapshot and send it to you.

Promoting Your Promotion

Now you're going to promote your contest. You can promote it in your brick-and-mortar store, on your own website and on the other social media platforms that you use. There are all kinds of ways that you can promote your contest but you do want to keep in mind that you have to let your followers know in a very clear fashion if you decide to use their videos later on in a future promotion.

Checking Your Contest Entries

The next step in the process is checking your contest entries. For example, if you had your users send you videos one of the things that you can do to make sure that you see all of the entries is to use a third-party program to view the videos and save them to your phone. You are probably aware by now that if you use Snapchat and someone sends you a video or a snap, it is going to self-destruct in no more than 10 seconds unless they build a story with it in which case it will be gone in 24 hours.

From there is just a matter of figuring out who the winner is in your promotion or however you designed it – with multiple winners or with everyone receiving some sort of promotional code – however you choose to create a fun and exciting promotion that your followers will like. If you can do this, you will find that the followers that you have will be much more apt to check out your snaps and videos as well as stories when you post them.

Chapter 15:

ALIGNING YOURSELF WITH NICHE INFLUENCERS ON SNAPCHAT

Chapter Fifteen: Aligning Yourself with Niche Influencers on Snapchat

One of the ways that you may not have considered marketing your company with Snapchat is to use niche influencers. This is actually a tried-and-true method of marketing and it is something that big companies do quite often. Some companies have partnered with YouTube stars in the past who work in the same niche as them – such is cosmetic companies pairing up with extremely popular makeup tutorial YouTubers – and so it is a very good way to market your company.

What are Niche Influencers?

So, what are niche influencers? They are people who have a lot of influence over a large number of potential customers within your own niche. Niche influencers often have large followings that go out and buy their recommended products and trust them implicitly. When it comes to anything that they use personally, followers will go out and buy that particular product in droves, which is why brands send popular YouTubers free samples of their products all the time.

Benefits of Using Niche Influencers

There are a lot of benefits to using niche influencers. For one thing, you are going to have a chance to entice their audience to come over to your particular company when they need a product or service that you provide. For another, the name of your company will be going around within circles that make up your industry.

How to Use Niche Influencers

So, how should use niche influencers? There are many creative ways that you can do this. Some people send them free samples of whatever products or services that they are selling – as long as that particular influencer is in your industry that is perfectly acceptable – and others do things like allowing a well-known person to take over a social media account. In fact that is something that is been quite a trend recently.

How to Find Niche Influencers

Finding niche influencers within your particular industry isn't all that difficult. You can use websites like Klout, Peer Index and Cred or any of the other barometers of influence that are out there. You can also check social media and find out who has a huge following within your particular industry. There are various ways to go about this depending on what social media platforms that you use but you definitely should check Twitter, Insta Graham, Pinterest and Facebook. Of course, you may be able to find out who the niche influencers are within your industry that are also on Snapchat.

Chapter 16:

MEASURING YOUR SUCCESS WITH SNAPCHAT

Chapter Sixteen: Measuring Your Success with Snapchat

So how do you measure your success with Snapchat? Knowing whether or not a campaign was successful, will depend on coming up with creative ways that you can figure out whether or not something worked. For example, if you did a Snapchat marketing campaign and you asked the users on that platform to do something on a different platform, then it would be very easy to measure your success – or at least the numbers. However, there is more to success than the numbers and we'll get into that here.

First, Let's Talk about the Numbers

Obviously, the numbers are important. But there is a great deal more to be aware of. Before you can get into any of that however, you need to know the numbers and so you are going to have to come up with some method of figuring out how many people you reached on Snapchat and how many of them took your call to action and actually follow through with signing up for an email list, posting a tweet with a certain hashtag or whatever particular method that you are using. You can make use of the Snapchat tools that were discussed in the chapter on analytics as well as your own methods of counting people that have responded.

Now, Let's Talk about the Demographics

So, you are going to have to figure out some way that you can get demographic information from the people that are responding to your marketing campaigns. Demographics are super important when it comes to campaigns because if you know what type of people have responded to a particular product or service, or advertising campaign, then you know how to improve it next time. Demographics can be difficult to get in the best way is probably to go with one of the companies that were discussed in the chapter on analytics because there is really no way to get that information with your own efforts.

Now, Let's Talk about User Response

The last thing that you want to measure is how the users felt about the particular marketing campaign that you did. You want to know what they thought of the campaign itself and also, you should try to find out whether they were happy to sign up for your mailing list because the offer was terrific or whether they were on the fence about it. Finding out how users responded to a particular marketing campaign can go a long way in helping you improve future marketing campaigns and get better responses.

Chapter 17:

LEARNING FROM OTHER BRANDS ON SNAPCHAT

Chapter Seventeen: Learning From Other Brands on Snapchat

You should definitely learn from other brands on Snapchat. There are several ways to do this but with the platform constantly evolving and with new marketing ideas coming all the time it can be a little time-consuming to keep up with everything. However you do want to make an effort to try to figure out what other companies are doing – particularly the biggest companies because those are going to be the easiest ones to find and will save you a little time. Figure out what other brands did and then come up with methods that work just as well. In this chapter, were going to come up with some ways that you can find out what other brands are up to and learn from them.

News Articles

If you follow marketing news, you are definitely going to find people talking about Snapchat. With 2 million active users per month there are a lot of people with their eye on this particular application who want to see where it is going – particularly since the company refused Facebook's offer. So if you look at the marketing news websites where you set up your new search for Snapchat you should build a find some great information on what some of the major brands are up to when it comes to Snapchat.

Ask Other People in the Industry

Another thing that you can do is ask other people that you know are in the industry. Regular communication with professionals like yourself that are within the same industry that you are in will allow you to share a great deal of information with each other that you might not have had on your own. People that are within your own industry are easy to find and unless they are direct competitor there probably going to be very happy to discuss their methods.

Follow Marketing Blogs That Are All about the Trends

Find some great marketing blogs that have good information and then sign up to get regular updates or an RSS feed from them. Bloggers will do quite a bit of research regularly and so they may be able to get information before you can on some of the trends that are going on in Snapchat. You can use Google search to find bloggers who concentrate particularly on Snapchat and on the marketing that goes with it.

Chapter 18:

INTEGRATING SNAPCHAT WITH YOUR SITE & SOCIAL MEDIA

Chapter Eighteen: Integrating Snapchat with Your Site & Social Media

Depending upon what type of site you have, adding Snapchat to it could be very easy or could be quite difficult. There are so many platforms out there now for creating a website and content management systems like WordPress are not the only players in the DIY world of website creation. In this chapter, were going to discuss how you can integrate Snapchat with your website and with your social media.

If you have a WordPress website being able to integrate Snapchat will depend upon the theme that you have. While all of the current themes definitely have places for Facebook, Twitter, Pinterest and others that are more well-known, not very many of the themes out there have automatic places where you can put your Snapchat information. However, you can put your Snapchat ID and even your QR code on the sidebar of your WordPress site by using a text widget.

If your website is built from scratch with HTML then you may have to get your web designer to create a place for your Snapchat QR code and for the user information that you want to post on your website. You should definitely put the QR code in the header of your homepage so that people can easily take a picture of it and try to follow you on Snapchat whenever they visit your website.

Integrating your Snapchat into your social media is going to take some creativity on your part. There really isn't any place that you can post your QR code and Snapchat information on Twitter. The only thing that you could do is replace your profile picture with your QR code but this is probably a bad idea for several reasons – one Twitter might not be happy that you're using a competing social media site's QR code on their site and Snapchat might not be happy about it either.

There is also the fact that you should have a decent profile picture on your Twitter account. One idea that may work on both Twitter and Facebook is putting your QR code within the background – in twitter that means the background that your tweets are sitting on and on Facebook you would have to put it in the larger header profile.

Just make sure that you aren't being obtrusive so that the social media website doesn't have to you about putting a QR code from a different social network onto their site – which they usually don't – and don't forget to remind people within your social media feeds as well as integrating it into the platform.

Conclusion:

Snapchat is one of the most interesting social platforms that is come around in a long time. The way that it allows users to communicate only through pictures and video is very interesting and it will be fascinating to see how the platform develops in the future. Marketing on Snapchat is something that people are starting to do more and more and companies are spending a significant portion of their marketing budget on speaking to those people who use Snapchat.

In this book, we've gone over some of the reasons that you should use this social media platform and even took you through the entire sign up process so you can get your account online. We also showed you how to create your QR code which you will be able to use on all kinds of things like your website, the wall of your brick-and-mortar business, other places you decide to put it like your business cards and even other social media platforms.

Some of the highlights of the other areas that were discussed in the book include: taking you through the process of building stories and showing you how you can get fans by using the stories as well as how you can get your initial following. There was also a great deal of information on using analytics and how you can use the numbers for Snapchat gives you to measure your own success. You can also use the analytics companies that are out there that promise to give you detailed information about your marketing efforts. Finally, we went over several ways that you can use Snapchat with other social media platforms and things like live events as well as give you some ideas on how to get followers – like using rand influencers.

It is our hope that the information in this book will allow you to start using Snapchat and be able to use all of the features successfully without any problems. While there is no guarantee that a marketing campaign on Snapchat will be successful, there must be a reason why so many companies are starting to use Snapchat to do marketing. Since other people have found a great deal of success and companies are spending three quarters of a million dollars a day just to be listed on the platform, odds are good that you will find success as well.

SNAPCHAT
MARKETING EXCELLENCE

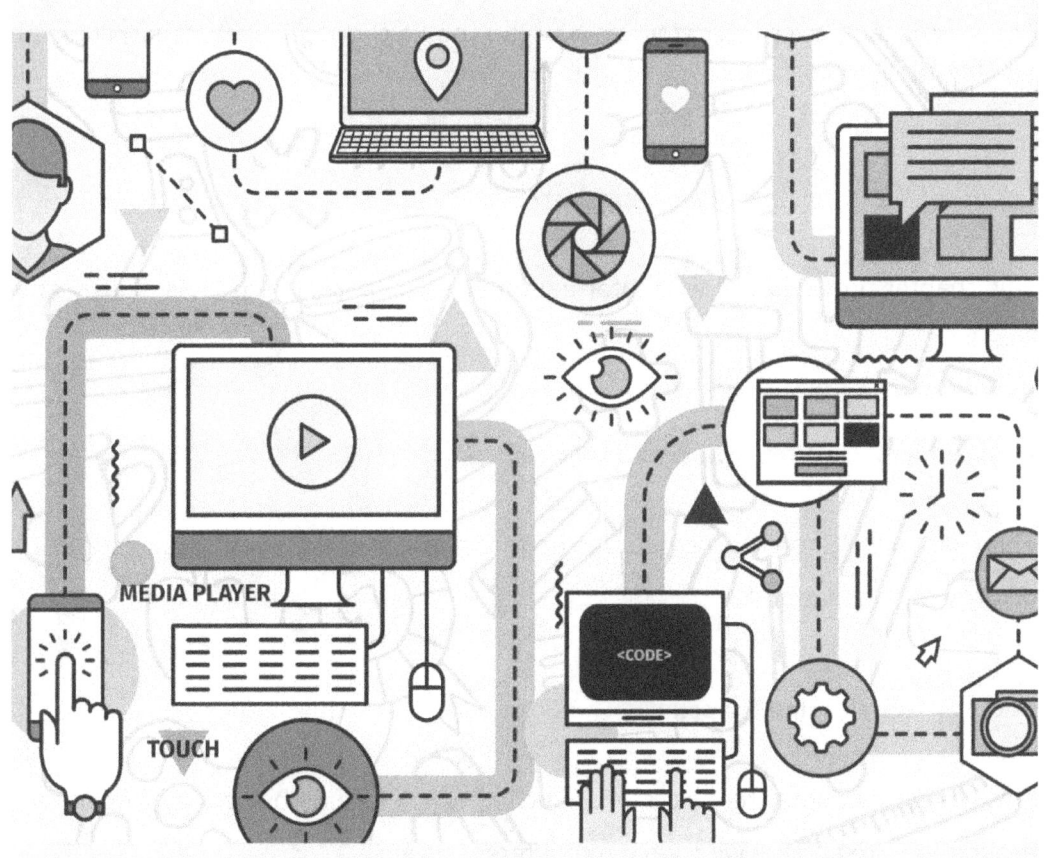

Snapchat Marketing Cheat Sheet

Here's a cheat sheet so that you can easily be able to go over the material in the book at a glance and make sure that you understand everything and that you haven't missed anything in your own efforts. We covered a lot of material, so here is a little about each chapter in the book.

Introduction: Why Snapchat Marketing?

The introduction gives you details on why you should choose Snapchat marketing for your business.

Chapter One: What exactly is Snapchat?

This chapter provides you with information about Snapchat, what it is exactly and how it works.

Chapter Two: Getting Your Brand on Snapchat

This chapter will show you how to sign up for Snapchat and get your business profile actually on the platform.

Chapter Three: Using Snapchat – The Basics

This chapter is about the basics of Snapchat, which include being able to navigate around the site and knowing what the different pages are for.

Chapter Four: Using Snapchat – Features Businesses Use the Most

This chapter teaches you how to use the integrated tools that Snapchat offers so that you can make your own QR code and get your logo on the site.

Chapter Five: Using Snapchat – Advanced Features

Chapter 5 goes over some of the more advanced features.

Chapter Six: Introduction to Marketing on Snapchat

This chapter will explain how you can use stories in Snapchat to market your products or services.

Chapter Seven: Getting Your Initial Following

Chapter 7 will teach you how to build your initial following and some tips on what not to do.

Chapter Eight: Building Fans through Stories

This chapter will show you how to build fans through the stories feature and teach you exactly how it works.

Chapter Nine: Discover – Snapchat's Partner Program

Chapter 9 is all about Snapchat's partner program which is called Discover.

Chapter Ten: Viewing Statistics

This chapter will teach you how you can view your statistics and analytics with Snapchat, and what to do if you want more detailed analytics.

Chapter Eleven: Using Snapchat at Live Events to get Followers

Live events can be a great way to get new followers on Snapchat as well as a way of getting current followers to come to your live events.

Chapter Twelve: Using Snapchat to Deliver Personal Content

You will learn here how to use Snapchat to do personal snaps that will actually help your business.

Chapter Thirteen: Give Followers an Inside Look

This chapter shows you how to use behind-the-scenes information to get followers.

Chapter Fourteen: Running Contests & Promotions on Snapchat

These are detailed instructions on how to run a contest or promotion on Snapchat.

Chapter Fifteen: Aligning Yourself with Niche Influencers on Snapchat

How influencers in your industry can get you followers.

Chapter Sixteen: Measuring Your Success with Snapchat

This chapter tells you how to know if you have been successful at your marketing efforts.

Chapter Seventeen: Learning From Other Brands on Snapchat

You can learn a lot from other brands. This chapter shows you where to find the information.

Chapter Eighteen: Integrating Snapchat with Your Site & Social Media

This chapter will help you use Snapchat with other social media and integrate it into your site.

SNAPCHAT
MARKETING EXCELLENCE

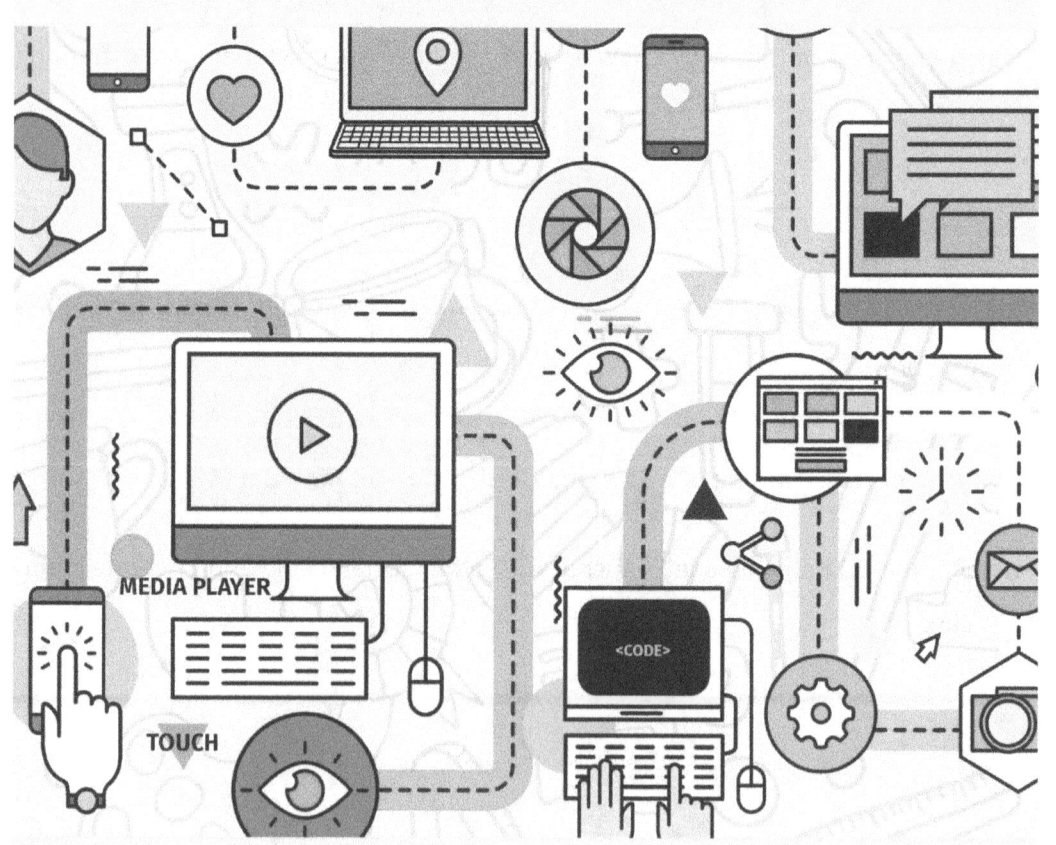

Snapchat Marketing Resource Sheet

If you want to know more about Snapchat marketing, there are a few things out there on the web that may be pretty valuable in teaching you what you need to know. This resource sheet is going to give you links to web resources in various categories, so that you can do further research after you finish the book.

Blogs to Follow that Talk about Marketing Trends

One of the things that is discussed in the later chapters of the book is that you need to understand what trends are happening so that you can use similar methods to get your own message out there. These are some of the blogs that have the best information on marketing trends.

http://blog.hubspot.com
http://blogs.adobe.com/digitalmarketing/
http://www.bryaneisenberg.com/

Websites to Visit so That You Can Get More Information on Snapchat Features

You may want to find out more about how to use Snapchat and you might even benefit from seeing screenshots of some of the things that you need to do with your account. That's why we've come up with some resources that will show you things like using Snapchat to post snaps, videos and stories as well as ones that walk you through the sign up process all the way from the very beginning to the end.

http://www.pcadvisor.co.uk/how-to/mobile-phone/how-use-new-snapchat-features-lenses-filters-trophies-buy-extra-replays-in-app-purchases-3515801/
http://blog.snapchat.com/

http://www.verizonwireless.com/mobile-living/tech-smarts/what-is-snapchat-how-to-use-new-features/

Sites That Measure the Reputation of Various Users on the Internet

If you are going to use influencers for your marketing then you are definitely going to want to check out some of the sites that measure the reputation of people. You can use the sites to figure out who has the reputation that you want and the followers that you would like to speak to.

www.klout.com

http://www.peerindex.com/

www.kred.com

Some of the Analytics Companies That Are Providing Analytics for Snapchat

Another thing that you might find useful, is a list of some of the companies out there that are providing services for Snapchat users on analytics and statistics. Snapchat has very little in the way of analytics, so if you want detailed information your best bet may be going with the third-party company. These companies offer analytic services for Snapchat.

http://blog.sumall.com/journal/metrics-dont-disappear-effectively-measure-snapchat-efforts.html

http://delmondo.co/primer-snapchat-analytics/

http://simplymeasured.com/blog/new-snapchat-analytics-report-from-simply-measured/

Snapchat Marketing Campaigns That Have Worked

If you have ever wanted to see what it was that made other companies marketing campaign successful, these articles will show you exactly what those companies did and how successful they were at it. You may be able to see these ideas in action and actually come up with your own ideas that will allow you to create a Snapchat marketing campaign has a much higher rate of success.

http://www.slideshare.net/simplify360/5-brilliant-snapchat-campaigns-1
http://keyhole.co/blog/top-5-snapchat-campaigns-by-innovative-brands/
http://www.postano.com/blog/the-15-best-snapchat-campaigns-of-2015
https://econsultancy.com/blog/66867-five-seriously-creative-snapchat-campaigns-and-their-results/
http://www.fastcocreate.com/3033793/how-12-brands-used-snapchat

Reasons to use Snapchat

If you didn't have enough information to allow you to choose Snapchat is one of the social media platforms that you will be using for marketing, here is some information that will allow you to see what some of the reasons that experts recommend for using Snapchat. If you are not already convinced, these will definitely convince you.

http://www.newsweek.com/5-reasons-use-snapchat-besides-reason-337485
http://mwpartners.com/snapchat/
http://blog.hootsuite.com/smart-ways-to-use-snapchat-for-business/
http://www.womenonbusiness.com/business-use-snapchat-marketing/
http://blog.hubspot.com/marketing/guide-to-using-snapchat-for-marketing

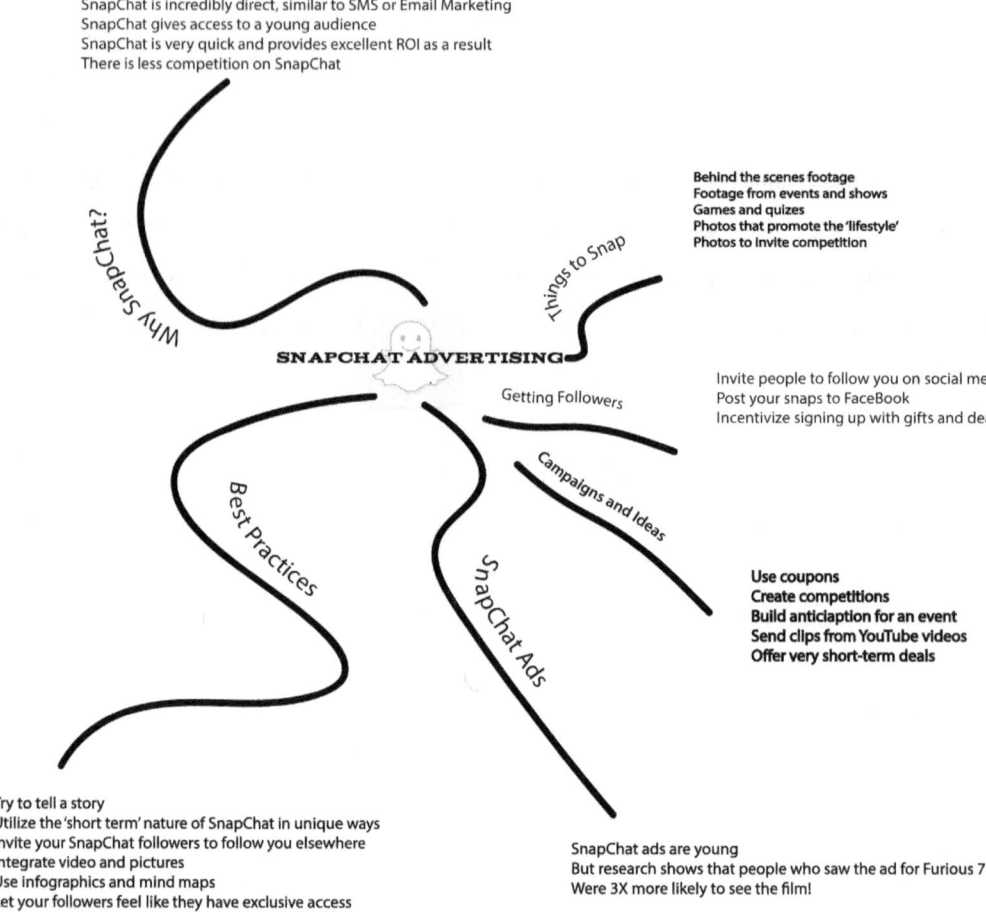

SNAPCHAT MARKETING CHEAT SHEET

Why SnapChat?
- SnapChat is incredibly direct, similar to SMS or Email Marketing
- SnapChat gives access to a young audience
- SnapChat is very quick and provides excellent ROI as a result
- There is less competition on SnapChat

Things to Snap
- Behind the scenes footage
- Footage from events and shows
- Games and quizzes
- Photos that promote the 'lifestyle'
- Photos to invite competition

Getting Followers
- Invite people to follow you on social media
- Post your snaps to FaceBook
- Incentivize signing up with gifts and deals

Campaigns and Ideas
- Use coupons
- Create competitions
- Build anticiaption for an event
- Send clips from YouTube videos
- Offer very short-term deals

SnapChat Ads
- SnapChat ads are young
- But research shows that people who saw the ad for Furious 7 Were 3X more likely to see the film!

Best Practices
- Try to tell a story
- Utilize the 'short term' nature of SnapChat in unique ways
- Invite your SnapChat followers to follow you elsewhere
- Integrate video and pictures
- Use infographics and mind maps
- Let your followers feel like they have exclusive access
- Treat them like VIPs!

www.ingramcontent.com/pod-product-compliance
Lightning Source LLC
Chambersburg PA
CBHW070331190526
45169CB00005B/1849